MIKE FINK

Adapted by **Stephen Krensky**

Illustrations by **Jeni Reeves**

On My Own

FOLKLORE

M Millbrook Press/Minneapolis

The illustrator wishes to thank Taci Campbell, William Meissner, and Bob Wiederaenders of the National Mississippi River Museum and Aquarium, Dubuque, IA. And thanks to the models: Douglas Schrum; Barbara and Michael Officer; Jeffrey Garner; Kory Kazimour; Traci, David, Kyra, and Derek Vercande; Rachel Hegseth; and Stuart Reeves.

Text copyright © 2007 by Stephen Krensky
Illustrations copyright © 2007 by Lerner Publishing Group, Inc.

Millbrook Press, Inc.
A division of Lerner Publishing Group, Inc.
241 First Avenue North
Minneapolis, MN 55401 U.S.A.

Website address: www.lernerbooks.com

Library of Congress Cataloging-in-Publication Data

Krensky, Stephen.
    Mike Fink / adapted by Stephen Krensky.
       p.   cm. — (On my own folklore)
    Summary: Relates the deeds of the frontiersman who became the King of the Keelboatmen on the Mississippi River
    ISBN-13: 978–1–57505–891–7 (lib. bdg. : alk. paper)
    ISBN-10: 1–57505–891–X (lib. bdg. : alk. paper)
    1. Fink, Mike, 1770-1823—Legends. [1. Fink, Mike, 1770-1823?—Legends.
2. Folklore—United States. 3. Tall tales.] I. Title.
PZ8.1.K8663Mik 2007
398.2'0973'02–dc22   2005010195

Manufactured in the United States of America
2 3 4 5 6 7 – DP – 12 11 10 09 08 07

For my nephew Danny, a rough-and-tumble kind of guy
—S.K.

To the memory of Dominic Legnini, a great
boatman and tall-tale teller
—J.R.

Mike Fink: A Folklore Hero

Maybe you have heard stories about Mike Fink. Well, there really was such a man. And he really did work on the keelboats and flatboats of the Ohio and Mississippi rivers. He was known as a fighter, a trapper, and a good shot with a rifle. He did some exploring too. Mike had so many adventures. People started to spin tales about him.

We call stories like Mike Fink's tall tales because everything in them is extra big, extra fast, and extra wild. And the truth in these stories might be just a bit stretched. The heroes and heroines in tall tales are as tall as buildings, as strong as oxen, or as fast as lightning. They meet with wild adventures at every turn. But that's okay because they can solve just about every problem that comes their way.

Tall tales may be funny and outsized. But they describe the life that many workers and pioneers shared. The people in these stories often have jobs that real people had. And the stories are always set in familiar places.

The first tellers of these tales may have known these people and places. Or they may have wished they could be just like the hero in the story. The stories were told again and again and passed from person to person. We call such spoken and shared stories folklore.

Folklore is the stories and customs of a place or a people. Folklore can be folktales like the tall tale. These stories are usually not written down until much later, after they have been told and retold for many years. Folklore can also be sayings, jokes, and songs.

Folklore can teach us something. A rhyme or a song may help us remember an event from long ago. Or it can be just for fun, such as a good ghost story or a jump-rope song. Folklore can also tell us about the people who share the stories.

People loved to tell stories about Mike Fink and the rivers he traveled. The real man was born around 1770 near the frontier post of Pittsburgh, Pennsylvania. He died near the mouth of the Yellowstone River in Montana around 1823. Mike Fink loved to tell tall tales. It's probably safe to say that his favorites were the ones that he told about himself.

On the River

Mike Fink was the best keelboater on the river.

And he was the first to admit it.

Some folks claimed Mike was really

half horse and half alligator.

Maybe he was, and maybe he wasn't.

Mike never said so himself.

But he didn't argue either.

It was said that Mike grew up
with two regular parents
in the wilds of western Pennsylvania.
But Mike declared that
his father was a hurricane
and his mother an earthquake.
Mike said he raised himself in the woods
with only the trees for company.

When Mike got older,
he decided it was time to see
a bit more of the world.
The best way to do that
was on the river.
So Mike went to work on a keelboat.

Keelboats made their way
up the Ohio and Mississippi rivers.
Their crews used long poles
to push the boats upstream.

Pretty soon Mike had his own boat
and crew to boss around.
Over time, he learned every bend
and sandbar in the river.
Sometimes the river moved things around,
just to see if it could catch him napping.
But Mike knew the river's tricks,
and he always paid attention.

Life on the river was sometimes slow,
so Mike tried to make it more exciting.
He would arm wrestle, leg wrestle,
or thumb wrestle anyone
who would take his challenge.
Sometimes nobody was handy.
So he would pick on an alligator or two
just to stay in shape.
Mike wasn't afraid to take chances
even if it meant getting knocked around.
He would jump down a waterfall
on a bet, riding the rapids
like a bucking bronco.

People were surprised that
he would risk his life for a few dollars.
But Mike wasn't worried.
He figured that
even if the river swallowed him up,
he would taste so bad that
it would spit him out again directly.
When Mike came to town,
there was no mistaking his arrival.
"Whoo-oop!" he bellowed.
"I'm the original iron-jawed,
brass-mounted, copper-bellied
corpse maker from the wild woods!"
Mike worked hard.
And he played hard.
Judging by the snores
that rattled windows for miles around,
he slept hard too.

The Hunt

Mike never expected to settle down.
But then he started hearing tales
of a gal named Peg.
News about her spread faster
than smoke on the wind.
Rumor had it she had fought a duel
with a thunderbolt,
escaping without a single scratch,
and that she had ridden an alligator
down the Mississippi,
singing "Yankee Doodle" on the way.

Mike set about courting Peg
as quick as he could find her.
Luckily for him,
Peg liked his rough-and-tumble ways.
As a surprise for her birthday,
Mike trained some alligators
to spell out her name.
After that, they got married
and settled down together.

Both Mike and Peg had hearty appetites.

So Mike did a lot of hunting

to keep food on the table.

It was said he could knock the saddle

off a horsefly at a hundred yards.

And that was with his eyes closed.

One time he was out hunting moose
and got separated from his friends.
Suddenly, they heard a great howl.
A moose burst out of the woods.
But it wasn't the moose
who had hollered.
It was Mike.
He was clinging to the antlers
for dear life.
The moose threw its antlers this way
and that.
But Mike held on tighter
than a cork in a bottle.
If he let go,
the moose would trample him for sure.

Now Mike's friends thought about
shooting the moose.
But they didn't want to hit Mike
by mistake.
He surely wouldn't take kindly to that.
So they just sat down to watch.

That moose bucked all day and night.
By the next morning, though,
the moose was a bit tired.
His snorting got louder.
And his knees began to wobble.
Mike finally hopped off
and backed away.
For a moment, he and the moose
just stared at each other.

Now Mike had been planning
to shoot the moose.
But now he had second thoughts.
A moose that stubborn and ornery—
it was like looking at himself
in the mirror.
Such a rare creature
clearly deserved to live.
So Mike brought the moose home
as a pet for Peg.
Mostly the moose just wandered
around outside their cabin,
scratching itself on the rough logs.
But sometimes Mike and Peg
hitched it to a wagon
and went for a wild ride.

A Scary Meeting

One day Mike met up
with the famous Davy Crockett.
"So you're Mike Fink, eh?" said Davy.
"Funny, I figured you to be bigger."
"You're about the size I expected,"
Mike answered, "seeing all the hot air
that's filling you up."
Having now met properly,
they each set to bragging a bit.
"One time," said Mike,
"I frightened a bear
just by frowning at it."

"Not bad," said Davy.

"But I knew a bear that ran away
after I only smiled."

Davy then started talking about his wife.

She was the strongest, bravest,
smartest wife east or west
of the Mississippi.

Now Mike had a fine opinion
of his own wife too.

He wasn't about to take this lying down.

He bet Davy a dozen wildcats
that he could frighten Mrs. Crockett
right out of her toenails.

"You're ugly, I admit," said Davy.

"But I don't think you're ugly enough
to do that."

Still, Davy took the bet
just to see what would happen.

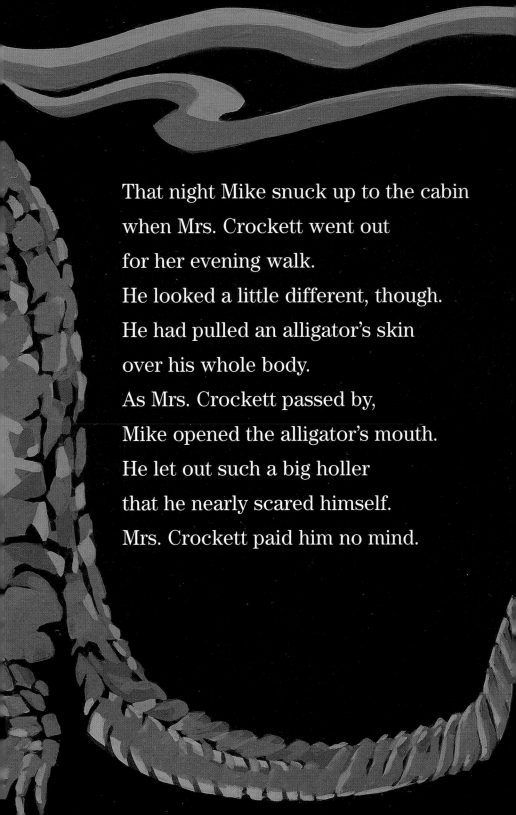

That night Mike snuck up to the cabin
when Mrs. Crockett went out
for her evening walk.
He looked a little different, though.
He had pulled an alligator's skin
over his whole body.
As Mrs. Crockett passed by,
Mike opened the alligator's mouth.
He let out such a big holler
that he nearly scared himself.
Mrs. Crockett paid him no mind.

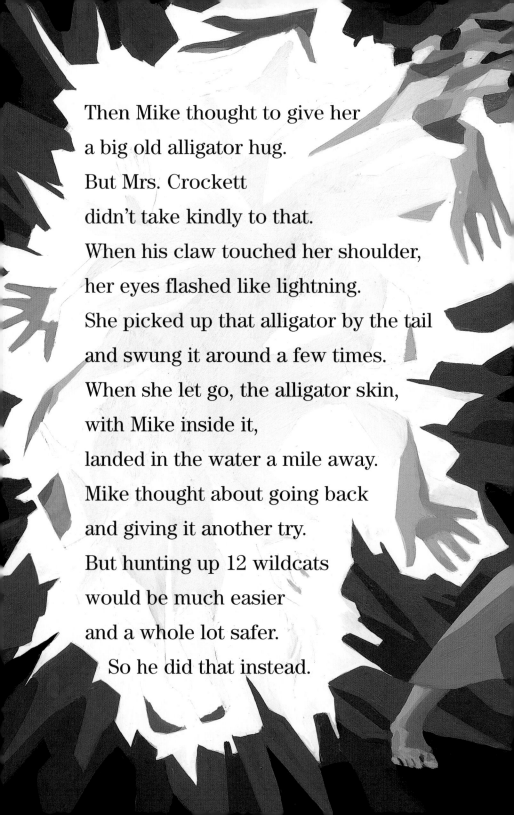

Then Mike thought to give her
a big old alligator hug.
But Mrs. Crockett
didn't take kindly to that.
When his claw touched her shoulder,
her eyes flashed like lightning.
She picked up that alligator by the tail
and swung it around a few times.
When she let go, the alligator skin,
with Mike inside it,
landed in the water a mile away.
Mike thought about going back
and giving it another try.
But hunting up 12 wildcats
would be much easier
and a whole lot safer.
  So he did that instead.

Not long after,
Mike went to the Crocketts for dinner.
Mrs. Crockett shook his hand
and said how pleased she was
to meet him.
"We're having one of our favorites
tonight," she said.

"Sounds good," said Mike.
"I'm hungry enough to eat a bear
without skinning it first."
Mrs. Crockett smiled.
"It's alligator stew.
My own recipe."
Mike just nodded
and smiled back as best he could.

The Race

There was a keelboater on the river
known as Powderkeg Pete.
He was called that
because of his short temper.
When he lost it, he turned beet red
and puffed up like a hot air balloon.
Now, Pete had lost his temper
many times when Mike
beat him out of a job.
Pete was looking to even the score.
So one day he challenged Mike to a race.
"Let's see who's got the fastest boat
on the river."

Mike laughed so hard at that
his teeth fell out.
It took him the better part of a week
to find them all
and put them back in the right places.

When he was done, Powderkeg Pete
made his challenge again.

"It wouldn't be fair," Mike protested.

"Not if you're a coward," said Pete.

"A coward!" shouted Mike.

"Name the time and place!
My crew will be ready."

The race drew a big crowd.
The starting pistol was fired.
Both teams set their poles
in the water
and started to push.

Suddenly, one of Mike's crew
felt his pole snap in his hand.
Then another pole snapped.
And a third.
"What's going on?" asked Mike.
His own pole had just snapped
like a matchstick.

"Someone's fiddled with our poles,"
said his crew.
"They've been partly cut through."
Mike looked up
to see Pete waving at him.
"See you at the finish line!"
Pete shouted.
"Don't worry. We'll wait."

If there was one thing
Mike Fink hated, it was a cheat.
He wasn't about to let
Powderkeg Pete get the best of him.
"Stand back!" he shouted.

Mike took a really deep breath.

Then he jumped into the river.

At first, nothing happened.

But then the boat began to move.

Faster and faster, it went.

"Mike's pushing us!" his men cried.

"We're catching up!"

Nobody could believe it,

especially Powderkeg Pete.

Mike's boat caught up with Pete's

around the last bend in the river.

Then it surged ahead

to cross the finish line first.

Everyone cheered.

They waited for Mike

to come back to the surface.

They waited and waited.

People were beginning to get a little nervous.
Finally, Mike's head poked up
out of the water.
"What took you so long?" they asked.
"Well," Mike said,
"I met up with a couple of alligators
who wanted me to join them for lunch."

"I turned down the invitation,
but they wouldn't take no for an answer."
Mike pounded his fists together.
"So I had to explain it to them."
He looked around.
"I've got some explaining to do
to Powderkeg Pete as well."
But Pete and his men were long gone.

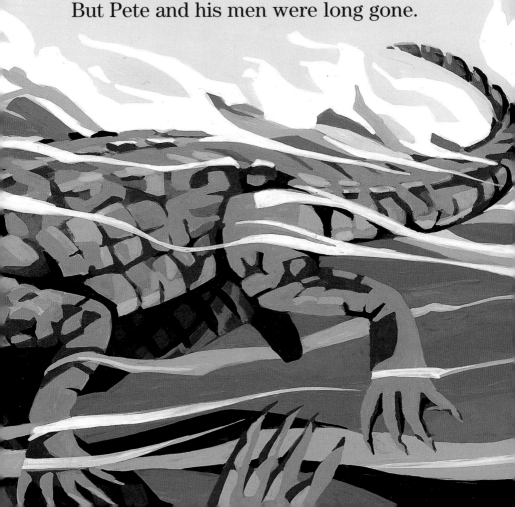

"Well," said one of the bystanders,
"I guess there's no question
who's king around here."
Mike Fink smiled, folding his arms.
"No question at all," he said.
And he remained
the king of the keelboaters
for a long time to come.